Chapter Resource File
with Answer Key

Holt Social Studies

World History

HOLT, RINEHART AND WINSTON
A Harcourt Education Company
Orlando • **Austin** • New York • San Diego • Toronto • London

Printed in the United States of America

ISBN 0-03-042304-X

5 6 7 082 08 07 06

Contents

Section 1

DIRECTIONS Use the two vocabulary words from the section (**communism** and **Vladimir Lenin**) to write a summary of what you learned in the section.

____

____

____

____

____

____

____

____

____

Section 2

Allies	Axis Powers	Cold War
genocide	Holocaust	dictatorship

DIRECTIONS Use the words in the word bank to write a summary of what you have learned.

Section 3

DIRECTIONS Write a word that has the same meaning as the term given.

1. ideologies ______________________
2. Korean War ______________________
3. Mikhail Gorbachev ______________________
4. Mohandas Gandhi ______________________
5. Ronald Reagan ______________________
6. terrorism ______________________
7. Vietnam War ______________________

MIKHAIL GORBACHEV

B. 1931

WHY HE MADE HISTORY Mikhail Gorbachev led the Soviet Union from 1985 to 1991. He helped end the Cold War by instituting extensive reform within the Communist government.

As you read the biography below, *think about how Mikhail Gorbachev's reforms led to the disbanding of the Soviet Union.*

VOCABULARY

glasnost openness

perestroika restructuring

Following World War II, relations between the United States and the Soviet Union were tense. This period of animosity between the two countries was called the Cold War. When Gorbachev became leader of the Soviet Union, he saw the devastating effects Communism had on the Soviet people. He sought to change the economy through **glasnost**, or openness, and **perestroika**, or restructuring. Gorbachev knew that reforming his government would mean repairing strained relations with the western world, particularly the United States.

Gorbachev's reforms gave the people of the Soviet Union more freedom than they had experienced in many years. Soviets were allowed to own their own businesses and enjoyed a greater freedom of speech. The reforms taking place in the Soviet Union were unprecedented and leaned more towards democracy than communism. In part due to these changes, Gorbachev met with President Reagan in 1986 to discuss the reduction of nuclear weapons. The meeting resulted in the signing of a treaty in 1987 to reduce the use of these powerful weapons.

In 1988, Gorbachev allowed the Eastern European nations under Soviet rule to control their own countries. This reform led to many revolutions, all peaceful but one, and eventually the Soviet Union collapsed. The fall of communism in Europe ended the Cold War. Gorbachev was awarded the Nobel Peace Prize in 1990 for his role in these major political changes.

Despite Gorbachev's reputation as somewhat of a hero in the United States, he became quite unpopular with the Soviet people. They blamed him for the hardships they endured after the end of the Soviet Union. As a result, Gorbachev did not win reelection. In late 2004, the leader of Russia, Vladimir Putin, replaced Gorbachev's electoral system of choosing regional leaders with a president-appointed system. Gorbachev criticized the move as a step backwards from democracy.

WHAT DID YOU LEARN?

1. Recall What were Gorbachev's ideas for changing the Soviet economy?

____

____

2. Evaluate Why do you think the people of the United States and the people of the former Soviet Union view Gorbachev differently?

____

____

ACTIVITY

Use what you know about communism and democracy to write a letter to Gorbachev congratulating him for winning the Nobel Peace Prize and telling why you believe he deserved this honor.

Name ______________________ Class ______________ Date ______________

Ronald Reagan

1911–2004

WHY HE MADE HISTORY Ronald Reagan was one of the most influential presidents of the United States. He witnessed great global changes during his time in office, most notably the end of the Cold War.

As you read the biography below, *think about how Ronald Reagan's ability to negotiate led to more peaceful relations between the United States and the Soviet Union.*

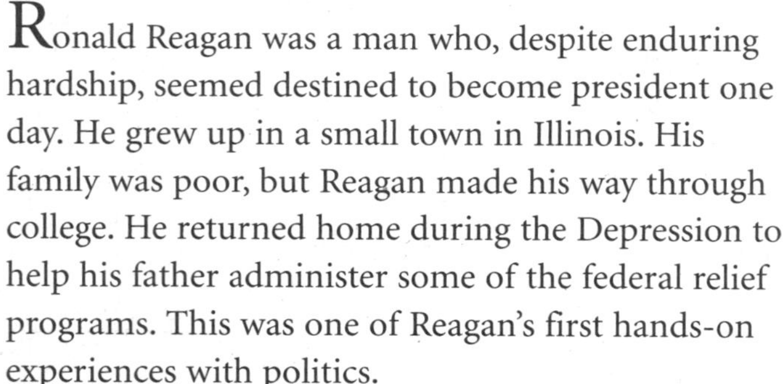

Ronald Reagan was a man who, despite enduring hardship, seemed destined to become president one day. He grew up in a small town in Illinois. His family was poor, but Reagan made his way through college. He returned home during the Depression to help his father administer some of the federal relief programs. This was one of Reagan's first hands-on experiences with politics.

Reagan did not start his political career right after college. In fact, he became a movie star in Hollywood, appearing in over fifty films. After a first marriage ended, he married actress Nancy Davis. Nancy became his lifelong companion. Reagan met Nancy during his tenure as president of the Screen Actors Guild, a role that deepened his interest in politics. At the time, the federal government accused many actors and motion picture companies of having ties to communism. Reagan defended the actors from the accusations. At that time, Reagan was a liberal Democrat. His political philosophy shifted, and he joined the Republican Party in 1962.

VOCABULARY

supply-side economics economic theory that stresses increased savings and investment along with lower taxes as a means to stimulate the economy

Cold War political tension and military rivalry between the United States and the Soviet Union after World War II

Reagan ran for governor of California and was elected for two terms. As governor, Reagan cut government spending and raised state taxes to try to reduce the state's deficit. After two unsuccessful attempts at getting the Republican presidential nomination, Reagan finally won the 1980 election for president of the United States.

As president, Reagan ignored political trends and instituted **supply-side economics**. He also increased military spending, in part to develop a space-based defense system. After his election to a second term as president, Reagan began to seek out the leader of the Soviet Union, Mikhail Gorbachev, in an effort to reduce the threat of nuclear war. Reagan, well known for his charm and ability to communicate, helped bring an end to the **Cold War**.

Reagan was one of the most popular presidents in U.S. history. In 1994, he announced he was battling Alzheimer's disease. Ronald Reagan died in 2004.

WHAT DID YOU LEARN?

1. **Recall** What was Reagan's theory of economics called?

   ____

   ____

2. **Evaluate** Reagan was known by many nicknames, including the "Great Communicator." How do you think his ability to communicate helped him in foreign relations? In your opinion, was this more or less effective than using military force? Explain your opinion.

   ____

   ____

ACTIVITY

Ronald Reagan delivered many powerful and important speeches throughout his life and especially during his presidency. Work with a partner to research three to five quotations from Reagan and explain their significance to the class.

FRANKLIN DELANO ROOSEVELT

1882–1945

WHY HE MADE HISTORY Franklin Delano Roosevelt was the 32nd president of the United States. He came to term during the Depression and helped restore the confidence of the American people.

As you read the biography below, *think about how Franklin Delano Roosevelt's optimism helped bring America out of the Great Depression.*

VOCABULARY

feminist belief in equality between the sexes

cunning crafty, tricky or sly

"The only thing we have to fear is fear itself." These words from Franklin Delano Roosevelt's inaugural speech set the tone for his plan to move America forward. Roosevelt's presidency began in the Great Depression. Many Americans were out of work and living in poverty. Roosevelt hoped to convey hope to the American people by helping to restore the economy.

In March 1933, 13 million people were unemployed. Banks were closed. Many people were hungry. Roosevelt worked with Congress to institute his New Deal programs, which helped to provide work for needy Americans. Part of Roosevelt's reforms included the establishment of the Social Security system, which provided financial support for the elderly and the poor. While most people agree that the policies established by Roosevelt helped move America through the Depression, others believe that those same policies helped prolong it.

Roosevelt was elected to his second term in 1936, a third term in 1940, and a fourth term in 1944. He is the only president to have been elected to more than two consecutive terms. The 22nd Amendment, added after Roosevelt's presidency, limits the number of terms a president can serve to two. Roosevelt's third and fourth terms were consumed greatly by World War II. Having offered every assistance except military involvement to those nations under attack from Germany and Japan, he led the nation into the war after the surprise Japanese attack on the U.S. naval base at Pearl Harbor in Hawaii on December 7, 1941.

Roosevelt died in April 1945, only a month before victory over Germany was announced in World War II, a war that he had fought so hard to win.

WHAT DID YOU LEARN?

1. Recall What event drew the United States into World War II?

____

____

2. Evaluate Do you think the 22nd Amendment is necessary? Why or why not?

____

____

ACTIVITY

Work with a partner to research one of the government agencies Roosevelt helped to establish. Examples include the Tennessee Valley Authority, Public Works Administration, and Works Progress Administration. Present your findings to the class.

The Grapes of Wrath

by John Steinbeck

ABOUT THE READING Many scholars consider *The Grapes of Wrath* to be one of the greatest novels ever written. The book gives a view of the life of American farm families driven from their homes during the Great Depression. The hardships the people faced as they journeyed west to California is captured in the story of the Joad family as they make their way across the hard land in search of work.

VOCABULARY

running board a step or footboard extending along each side of a vehicle

As you read the passage below, *think about how the families' lives were changed by the need to travel across the country with little food and money.*

In the morning the tents came down, the canvas was folded, the tent poles tied along the **running board**, the beds put in place on the cars, the pots in their places. And as the families moved westward, the technique of building up a home in the evening and tearing it down with the morning light became fixed; so that the folded tent was packed in one place, the cooking pots counted in their box. And as the cars moved westward, each member of the family grew into his proper place, grew into his duties; so that each member, old and young, had his place in the car; so that in the weary, hot evenings, when the cars pulled into the camping places, each member had his duty and went to it without instruction: children to gather wood, to carry water; men to pitch the tents and bring down the beds;

What kind of effect do you think living a migrant life might have on a family used to a farm home ?

____

____

Source: ***Viking Penguin, a division of Penguin Group (USA) Inc.:*** From *The Grapes of Wrath* by John Steinbeck. Copyright 1939 and renewed © 1967 by John Steinbeck.

women to cook the supper and to watch while the family fed. And this was done without command. The families, which had been units of which the boundaries were a house at night, a farm by day, changed their boundaries. In the long hot light, they were silent in the cars moving slowly westward; but at night they integrated with any group they found.

What does the last sentence tell you about how the people were feeling as they traveled westward?

____

____

ANALYZING LITERATURE

1. **Main Idea** What do you think was different in the daily lives of these families from what they had been used to?

____

____

2. **Critical Thinking: Drawing Inferences** Why was it important for each family member to be responsible for certain tasks? What purpose might this have served?

____

____

ACTIVITY

Imagine you are traveling with your family in search of work in California during the Depression. Create a journal entry about your travels and how you are feeling having left your home for life on the road.

"We Shall Fight on the Beaches" by Winston Churchill, June 4, 1940

ABOUT THE READING Winston Churchill, Britain's Prime Minister during World War II, is considered one of the greatest speechmakers of all time. He made the following speech after the Allies had suffered a great defeat at the hands of German forces. He uses his gifts as a speaker to reassure the British people that England will not be invaded and to encourage them to keep up the good fight.

VOCABULARY

tyrants evil rulers

outlandish odd

odious hateful

apparatus tools

subjugated dominated, under enemy control

As you read, *note how Churchill uses rhetorical devices, such as repetition, to convince his audience. What other techniques does he use to appeal to his audience's pride?*

. . . Turning once again, and this time more generally, to the question of invasion, I would observe that there has never been a period in all these long centuries of which we boast when an absolute guarantee against invasion, still less against serious raids, could have been given to our people. In the days of Napoleon the same wind which would have carried his transports across the Channel might have driven away the blockading fleet. There was always the chance, and it is that chance which has excited and befooled the imaginations of many Continental **tyrants**. Many are the tales that are told. We are assured that novel methods will be adopted, and when we see the originality of malice, the ingenuity of aggression, which our enemy displays, we may certainly prepare

An invasion of England or serious raids has always been possible.

We are certain that original methods will be used. When we see our enemy's originality of evil and the creativity of aggression, we must prepare ourselves for all kinds of evil doings.

From "I Expect Worse to Come . . ." from speech by Winston Churchill, begun at 3:40 p.m, ended at 4:15 p.m, 4 June 1940 from *Hansard*, columns 787–796. Copyright 1940 by The House of Lords and the House of Commons. Reproduced by permission of **Hansard**.

ourselves for every kind of novel stratagem and every kind of brutal and treacherous maneuver. I think that no idea is so **outlandish** that it should not be considered and viewed with a searching, but at the same time, I hope, with a steady eye. We must never forget the solid assurances of sea power and those which belong to air power if it can be locally exercised.

I have, myself, full confidence that if all do their duty, if nothing is neglected, and if the best arrangements are made, as they are being made, we shall prove ourselves once again able to defend our Island home, to ride out the storm of war, and to outlive the menace of tyranny, if necessary for years, if necessary alone. At any rate, that is what we are going to try to do. That is the resolve of His Majesty's Government—every man of them. That is the will of Parliament and the nation. The British Empire and the French Republic, linked together in their cause and in their need, will defend to the death their native soil, aiding each other like good comrades to the utmost of their strength. Even though large tracts of Europe and many old and famous States have fallen or may fall into the grip of the Gestapo and all the **odious apparatus** of Nazi rule, we shall not flag or fail. We shall go on to the end, we shall fight in France, we shall fight on the seas and oceans, we shall fight with growing confidence and growing strength in the air, we shall defend our Island, whatever the cost may be, we shall fight on the beaches, we shall fight on the landing grounds, we shall fight in the fields and in the streets, we shall fight in the hills; we shall never surrender, and even if, which I do not for a moment believe, this Island or a large part of it were **subjugated** and starving, then our Empire beyond the seas, armed and guarded by the British Fleet, would carry on the struggle, until, in God's good time, the New World, with all its power and might, steps forth to the rescue and the liberation of the old.

WHAT DID YOU LEARN?

1. Why do you think that Churchill says that invasion is always possible? Do you think he was wise to do so? Why or why not?

____

____

2. How does Churchill try to reassure his audience? Do you think he is successful? Why or why not?

____

____

3. How does Churchill appeal to his audience's pride in the speech?

____

____

Diary Entry of Private Sidney Williamson, Royal Warwickshire Regiment, July 1, 1916 (writing at the Battle of Somme)

ABOUT THE READING This diary entry is an example of the terrors of trench warfare. The Battle of Somme in France was one of the deadliest battles for the British during World War I. For a week before attacking, the British bombed German lines. They were confident of victory. However, the Germans simply moved underground and waited. On the first day of battle, July 1, 1916, eleven British divisions walked towards the German lines. The Germans began shooting their machine guns, and by the end of the day, 40,000 British soldiers were wounded, and 20,000 were dead.

VOCABULARY

lull pause

As you read, *note the soldier's description of battle. What is the soldier's attitude toward the subject? What images stand out?*

Diary: 1 July 1916

It was a lovely bright morning, but the feelings of the men were tense. We had breakfast at 5.00 a.m., afterwards the officers were going round to see all the men and have a talk with us. The shelling was terrific and the Germans started to shell our lines. At 7.20 a mine was exploded under the German trenches. An officer detailed me and another soldier standing by me to carry forward with us a box containing a signaling lamp. At 7.30 a.m. whistles

Diary entry 1 July 1916 "Private Sidney Williamson, 1/8th Battalion, Royal Warwickshire Regiment" from "the First World War 1914–1918" from *The Mammoth Book of War Diaries and Letters: Life on the Battlefield in the Words of the Ordinary Soldier, 1775–1991*, edited by Jon E. Lewis. Copyright © by **The Estate of Sidney Williamson.** Reproduced by permission of the copyright holder.

were blown and the attack started. What did I see! . . . lines of soldiers going forward as though on parade in line formation. Just "over the top" the soldier helping me with the box stopped and fell dead. I had to go on but without the box. Lt. Jones was the next officer I was to see fall, then CSM Haines was calling for me, he had been wounded. I reached the first German line and dropped into it where there were many German dead. The battlefield was nothing but shell holes and barbed wire, but now I noticed many dead and dying, and the lines of soldiers was not to be seen. With no officers or NCO near I felt alone but still went from shell hole to shell hole. . . Things were now getting disorganized and at this point we could not go any further. The machine-gun was deadly. And our bombs had all been used up. The Colonel of the Seaforths . . . told us to dig ourselves in and eventually there must have been 50 or 60 men at this spot, and it all started from the one small shell hole Cpl Beard and myself were first in.

Now there was a **lull** in the fighting till 3.0 p.m. At one time a shout went up that we were surrounded by Germans, but they were Germans running from the dugouts in the first line and giving themselves up. I do not think they made it.

With Cpl. Beard we started to get back to our lines shell hole by shell hole, but we soon got parted. I managed to reach the British lines at 7.30 p.m. but the sight that met my eyes was terrible. Hundreds of dead soldiers were everywhere, and the Germans kept up their heavy shelling.

WHAT DID YOU LEARN?

1. The soldier witnesses terrible death and destruction. Why do you think he uses such a matter-of-fact tone to tell what he saw?

____

____

2. What image or images stood out to you as you read? What thoughts or feelings did they bring to mind?

____

____

3. This solder continues moving toward the enemy even as many of his fellow soldiers fall. Do you think he considers himself to be a hero? Why or why not?

____

____

The Alliance System

By 1914, European countries feared each other's growing armies. They began to create new alliances with other countries in order to protect themselves. Two different alliances were formed. Germany, Austria-Hungary and Italy were part of the Triple Alliance. Russia, Great Britain, and France belonged to the Triple Entente. Several countries, however, remained neutral. Examine the map below, and answer the questions that follow.

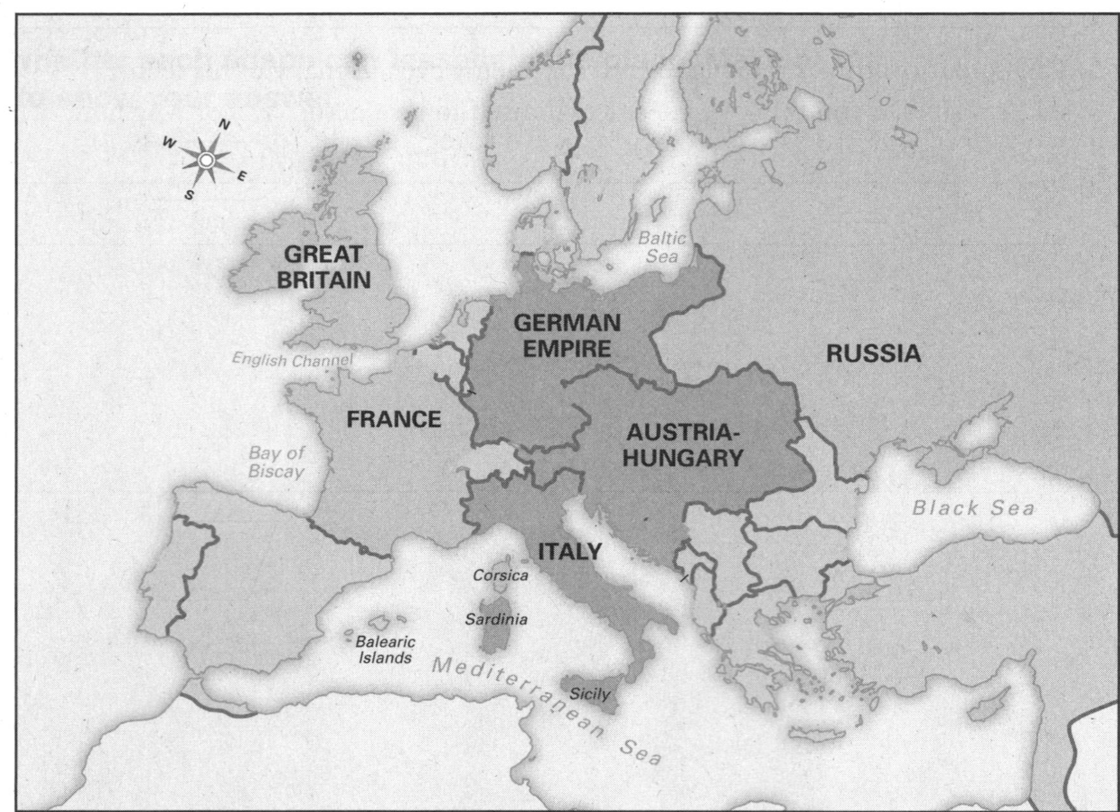

MAP ACTIVITY

1. On the map, label the European nations that were neutral in 1914.
2. Use a light color to shade in all of the neutral countries.
3. What sea is east of Great Britain? Label it on the map.
4. What ocean is west of France? Label it on the map.
5. Update the map legend to reflect the colors you added to the map.

ANALYZING MAPS

1. **Region** Which countries belonged to the Triple Alliance?

____

____

2. **Region** Which countries belonged to the Triple Entente?

____

____

3. **Place** How do you think a war on the continent of Europe might affect a country such as Great Britain, which is located on an island?

____

____

4. **Location** What is the name of the neutral country that shared borders with one country in the Triple Alliance, one country in the Triple Entente, and two neutral countries?

____

____

5. **Human-Environment Interaction** How do you think remaining neutral would affect a country like Switzerland and its people?

____

____

____

Understanding Historical Interpretation

LEARN THE SKILL

Historians look at facts as best they can, then interpret those facts to tell the story of history. Good historians gather facts and let those facts lead them to conclusions. A biased historian might only use facts that support a predetermined view of history. In any case, two good historians might look at the same data and come away with somewhat different ideas about what happened and why it did. Readers must be aware that history is always someone's interpretation. We must make allowances for human differences and the possibility of bias.

Interpretations of history also change over time. Sometimes this is because new discoveries bring to light information that earlier historians did not have. Sometimes a society's sense of what is important changes and historians modify their interpretations of history to reflect new social interests or beliefs. In the early 1800s, some Americans felt that slavery was normal and natural. By the 1900s, almost no one felt that way. Works of history came to reflect those new beliefs.

PRACTICE AND APPLY THE SKILL

In your textbook, read the section entitled "The Cold War." It is sometimes said that history is written by the winners. It is certainly true that histories written in the United States and those written in the Soviet Union differed substantially when discussing the same periods or conflicts.

Write two paragraphs explaining why some people say that "History is written by the winners." Include examples that might highlight the differences between the way historians in the United States and historians in Russia write about the Cold War.

Cover Story

Choose an event or person from the time period that would make a good cover story for a magazine. Then, write a short article for your cover story.

PREWRITING

1. **Taking Notes on Important People** Make a chart like the one below. In the first column, list some of the people who played key roles during World War I. In the second column, tell what these people accomplished. One row has been filled in to get you started.

Important Person	Accomplishments
Woodrow Wilson	• Had a plan to promote democracy and prevent future war • Had idea for a League of Nations, where countries could solve problems peacefully

2. **Taking Notes on Important Events** Make a list of the key events of World War II. For each event, write a sentence about the important people who were involved with that event. Be sure to mention the leaders of the Allies and the Axis Powers.

3. **Choosing a Topic** List some of the people and events you read about in this section. Then, look back over all of your notes, and choose a person or event to make the subject of your magazine cover story.

WRITING

4. Writing Your Cover Story Follow these steps to write your cover story. First, choose an event or person to write about. Remember that cover stories help sell magazines. Which story will be most intriguing to you readers? Then, write your story. Include an introductory sentence and facts and details about your subject. Explain why the subject was important enough to be featured on the front page.

PICTURE IT!

When you are finished with your cover story, create a magazine cover! Look at some news magazine covers, such as Time and Newsweek, for ideas. Then, create your own cover. Use a bold, colorful font for the title of the magazine. Find a picture that illustrates your story and grabs your readers' attention. Then, include a statement or question to get readers interested in your cover story.

EVALUATING AND PROOFREADING

1. Evaluating Your Cover Story Does your cover story do a good job of telling about a person or event? Use the questions below to evaluate and revise your cover story.

Rubric

- Is your story important and intriguing enough to be a cover story?
- Does your cover story begin with an introduction to the person or event?
- Does your story include important facts about your subject?
- Does your story show your reader why your subject was important?

2. Proofreading Your Cover Story Last, check the following:

- Capitalization and spelling of all proper names and places
- Punctuation, grammar, and spelling

Name ______________________ Class ______________ Date ______________

Global Challenges — Chapter Review

BIG IDEAS

1. World War II, fought from 1914 to 1918, caused terrible destruction and changed Europe forever.
2. World War II, the most destructive conflict in history, was followed by the Cold War between the United States and the Soviet Union.
3. Since World War II, countries around the world have gone through dramatic political, economic, and technological changes.

REVIEWING VOCABULARY, TERMS, AND PEOPLE

Use the clues provided to fill in the crossword puzzle below

Across

3. The man who led a nonviolent independence movement in India.
5. Systems of beliefs. Two examples are communism and capitalism.
6. The economic and political system created in the Soviet Union after the Russian Revolution.

Down

1. The deliberate destruction of a people.
2. A political philosophy based on nationalism and a strong government.
4. The Nazi genocide of the Jewish people during World War II

COMPREHENSION AND CRITICAL THINKING

Read each pair of people or events. Circle the one that occurred first.

1. World War II OR Cold War

2. Mikhail Gorbachev OR Vladimir Lenin

3. increased nationalism OR end of colonialism

4. Treaty of Versailles OR World War I

REVIEWING THEMES

Using the lists below, determine what theme from history they have in common.

Themes

geography	politics	economics	technology and innovation	society and culture	religion

______________________ **1.** global economy, Internet, cable TV networks, video conferences, mobile phones, email

______________________ **2.** communism, fascism, ideologies, nationalism, imperialism, capitalism

REVIEW ACTIVITY: THE FIVE W'S GAME

Create a game about important people, events, and ideas described in the chapter. The game can be a board game, card game, or quiz show type of game, but it must use questions that start with one of the five W's: who, what, where, when, and why. Write at least three questions for each "W" word. Include instructions on how to play, how to keep score, and an answer key. Use the ideas below to help you write questions for your game.

leaders	events	alliances	conflicts
countries	nationalism	ideologies	colonialism
conflicts	imperialism	revolutions	terrorism
technology	economy	governments	challenges

Vocabulary Builder Section 1

Answers will vary but one example is:
This section is about World War I. The war started in the summer of 1914 in Europe. One of the causes of World War I was nationalism. People were willing to go to war to prove that their country was superior to other nations. Some nations wanted to rule their own nation instead of having someone else rule them. Imperialism, or competing for control of colonies, also added to Europe's problems. European nations also began to build large armies in the early 1900s. All of these things began to cause European nations to fear each other, so they began to make new alliances to protect themselves.

World War I actually started after a Serbian nationalist killed Archduke Francis Ferdinand, who was the heir to the Austro-Hungarian throne. His wife was also killed. Austria-Hungary and Serbia were neighbors. Seeking revenge, Austria-Hungary declared war on Serbia. The alliance systems that had been established in Europe split Europe into two warring sides. The Central Powers were led by Austria-Hungary and Germany. The Allies, including Great Britain, France, and Russia, were against the Central Powers. Eventually other countries joined the two sides.

The United States joined the war in 1917. With the added help from the United States, the Allies finally won World War I. The Treaty of Versailles ended the war.

One result of World War I was the Russian Revolution. In 1917 Czar Nicholas II, the ruler of Russia, was forced to give up power. A group in Russia, the Bolsheviks, grew in strength. The Bolsheviks were supporters of communism. Communism is an economic and political system in which the government owns all businesses and controls the economy. The Bolshevik leader was Vladimir Lenin. Under Lenin, the Bolsheviks overthrew the new government and created the world's first Communist state.

Vocabulary Builder Section 2

Students' summaries will vary but should reflect an understanding of the terms and their relationship to the content of the chapter.

Vocabulary Builder Section 3

1. systems of beliefs; each side believes its economic and political systems are best
2. war between North Korea and South Korea; 1950 war in Asia
3. a Soviet leader; started reform movements to help the economy of the Soviet Union
4. led an independence movement in India in the 1920s and 1930s; led nonviolent protests
5. president of the United States; expanded U.S. military forces and weapons in the 1980s
6. criminal activity involving the use of violence to create fear and to push for political change; acts include shootings, bombings, kidnappings, and hijackings
7. war between North and South Vietnam; war began when communist North Vietnam attempted to reunite the country.

Biography Mikhail Gorbachev

WHAT DID YOU LEARN?

1. Gorbachev believed in openness and restructuring, known as glasnost and perestroika.
2. Accept reasonable answers.

Biography Ronald Reagan

WHAT DID YOU LEARN?

1. Reagan instituted supply-side economics.
2. Possible answer: Reagan's ability to communicate helped him seek more peaceful ways of dealing with the Soviet Union. I think this was more effective than military force because Reagan's willingness to talk about the issues represented an openness to cooperation. It also helped avoid a possible war.

Biography Franklin Delano Roosevelt

WHAT DID YOU LEARN?

1. The Japanese attack on Pearl Harbor on December 7, 1941
2. Accept reasonable answers.

Literature

ANALYZING LITERATURE

1. Answers will vary. Sample answer: I think that almost everything in the family's daily routine was changed. For instance they had to build their home every night and then take it down the next day. Kids in the family probably did their chores without being asked because everybody had a job to do if the family was going to make it.
2. Sample answer: It was important for everyone to be responsible for certain tasks so that way all the tasks got done. It was also important so the family members would know who to check with to make sure something had been done. It sounds like that for the family to survive, everybody had to pitch in and help and everybody had to develop a sense of responsibility.

ACTIVITY

Answers will vary. Accept all reasonable journal entries.

Primary Source "We Shall Fight on the Beaches" by Winston Churchill, June 4, 1940

WHAT DID YOU LEARN?

1. Possible response: Churchill probably says that invasion is possible to show that he is being honest with his audience. He was wise to do so to gain his audience's trust.
2. Possible response: He tries to reassure them by reminding them of the England's sea and air power and by saying that if everyone is diligent, the country will be safe. He is successful in reassuring them because he shows confidence that victory is possible.
3. He appeals to their pride by saying that England will fight whenever and wherever necessary to win.

Primary Source Diary Entry of Private Sidney Williamson, Royal Warwickshire Regiment, July 1, 1916 (Writing at the Battle of Somme)

WHAT DID YOU LEARN?

1. Possible responses: He was in shock. He had been fighting so long that he had become hardened to the sights of war.
2. Possible response: The image of the man carrying the box falling dead and the soldier having to keep going without him stood out. It made me feel sad to think of the soldier watching his fellow soldiers die.
3. Possible response: He probably doesn't think of himself as a hero. He describes his experiences that day in a unemotional way and doesn't give himself credit for strength or bravery.

History and Geography

MAP ACTIVITY

1. Albania, Belgium, Bulgaria, Denmark, Greece, Luxembourg, Montenegro, Netherlands, Norway, the Ottoman Empire, Portugal, Romania, Serbia, Spain, Sweden, and Switzerland should be labeled.
2. Colors will vary.
3. North Sea should be labeled.
4. Atlantic Ocean should be labeled.

ANALYZING MAPS

1. German Empire, Austria-Hungary, Italy
2. Great Britain, France, Russia
3. Answers will vary, but may mention that Great Britain could be attacked by sea or lose trading partners.
4. Romania
5. Students' answers will vary but should include that remaining neutral would bring new challenges to Switzerland. Surrounded by feuding nations, it might be pressured into siding with either alliance. The people of Switzerland were probably thankful of not losing their family members to the war but fearful of the feuding nations.

Social Studies Skills

PRACTICE AND APPLY THE SKILL

Students' answers will vary but should reflect some awareness of the ways by which society's values are displayed in histories. They might write about how open societies encourage accurate histories by making information more available. Students should include examples of how historians in Russia might emphasize or select certain information while American historians might select or emphasize other information.

Chapter Review

REVIEWING VOCABULARY, TERMS, AND PEOPLE

1. genocide
2. fascism
3. Gandhi
4. Holocaust
5. ideologies
6. communism

COMPREHENSION AND CRITICAL THINKING

1. World War II
2. Vladimir Lenin
3. increased nationalism
4. World War I

REVIEWING THEMES

1. technology and innovation
2. politics

REVIEW ACTIVITY: THE FIVE W'S GAME

Students' games should include questions that cover key concepts, terms, events, and people described in the chapter. Higher-quality products will encompass a greater number of concepts described in the chapter, with coverage of the main ideas of each section.